W9-AEY-280

Carmelo Anthony

By Jon M. Fishman

AMAZING ATHLETES

Lerner Publications Company • Minneapolis

Lerner Publications Company
A division of Lerner Publishing Group, Inc.
241 First Avenue North
Minneapolis, MN 55401 U.S.A.

Website address: www.lernerbooks.com

Library of Congress Cataloging – in – Publication Data

Fishman, Jon M.
    Carmelo Anthony / by Jon M. Fishman.
      pages cm. — (Amazing athletes)
    Includes index.
    ISBN 978–1–4677–2062–5 (lib. bdg. : alk. paper)
    ISBN 978–1–4677–2064–9 (eBook)
    1. Anthony, Carmelo, 1984—Juvenile literature. 2. Basketball players—United States—
Biography—Juvenile literature. I. Title.
GV884.A58.F57 2014
796.323092—dc23 [B]   2013003031

Manufactured in the United States of America
1 – BP – 7/15/13

TABLE OF CONTENTS

Carmelo Anthony *(right)* goes around DeQuan Jones of the Orlando Magic.

"WHATEVER IT TAKES"

New York Knicks **forward** Carmelo Anthony drove to the basket. DeQuan Jones of the Orlando Magic ran with him. Jones tried to keep Carmelo from scoring. But Carmelo rolled the ball into the basket. The **referee** called a **foul** on Jones.

Carmelo and the Knicks were playing against the Magic in Orlando on January 5, 2013. **Defenders** like Jones had been trying to stop Carmelo from scoring since he joined the National Basketball Association (NBA) in 2003–2004. Few players can stop him. Carmelo is one of the best scorers in the NBA.

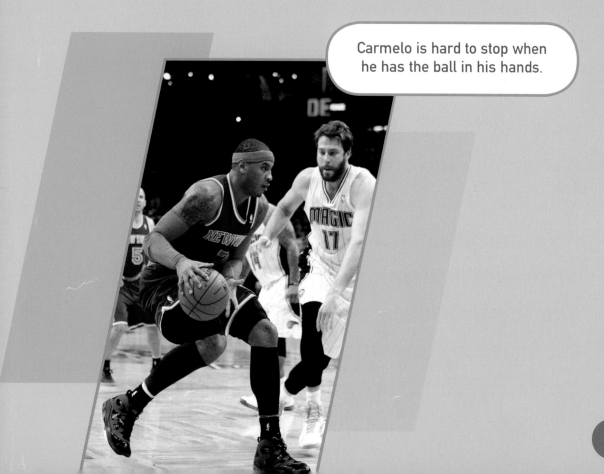

Carmelo is hard to stop when he has the ball in his hands.

Carmelo takes a shot against the Magic.

Carmelo made his **free throw**. The game was tied, 79–79. But the Knicks would score only once more in the third quarter. With one quarter to go the Magic had the lead, 89–81.

New York coach Mike Woodson knew it would be tough for his team to win in Orlando. "It's hard to win on the road, I don't care who you play," Woodson said.

Amar'e Stoudemire scored five points for the Knicks at the beginning of the fourth quarter. Then Carmelo made a **layup**. The Knicks continued to score while the Magic struggled. Carmelo made basket after basket.

He made another free throw with just 23 seconds left on the clock. The Knicks won the game, 114–106.

Carmelo plays his best when the game is on the line. He scored 16 points in the fourth quarter. The Magic scored only 17 points in the same quarter.

Carmelo married La La Vazquez in New York in 2010. The couple has a son named Kiyan.

Fans cheer for Carmelo and the Knicks.

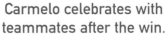

Carmelo celebrates with teammates after the win.

Coach Woodson was proud of his team. "We've been down before and we always seem to come back," the coach said. "Tonight wasn't any different." Carmelo ended the game with 40 points. He also had six **rebounds** and six **assists**. "Doing whatever it takes to win a game," Carmelo said. "That's what we did."

Brooklyn is a **borough** of New York City.
The city is made up of five boroughs.

MELO

Carmelo Kyam Anthony was born in Brooklyn, New York, on May 29, 1984. His family called him Melo. His mother's name is Mary. His father's name was also Carmelo. Carmelo has two older brothers named Wilford and Robert. He has an older sister named Daphne. His older sister Michelle died in 2010.

The Anthony family lived in the Red Hook neighborhood in Brooklyn. Red Hook is the largest group of public homes in the city. Most people who live there don't have much money. Carmelo's father died of cancer when the future basketball star was just two years old.

Mary moved the family to Baltimore, Maryland, when Carmelo was eight years old. They lived in a tough neighborhood on

Baltimore is the largest city in Maryland.

Myrtle Avenue. Drug use and violence were common in the area. But Carmelo stayed out of trouble. "He was always an excellent student," said his sixth-grade teacher. "Whenever he got into trouble, it was something small like talking in class."

Carmelo had a knack for sports. He wanted to be the pitcher when he played baseball. He was also a good **wide receiver** in football. But basketball was his favorite sport. He had a talent for putting the ball through the hoop. "He could always score the ball," said youth basketball coach Kevin McClain. "That's one thing you never need to worry about [with] Carmelo."

Carmelo did have one thing to worry about when he was young. "Between the ages of 6 and 13, I had trouble breathing, let alone running up and down the court," Carmelo wrote. "**Asthma** squeezed my lungs glove-tight." By high school, Carmelo's asthma attacks were behind him.

Carmelo was tall and skinny for a teenager. He was almost six feet tall. He weighed just 120 pounds. He didn't make the **varsity** team as a freshman at Towson Catholic High School near Baltimore. But a lot would change for the 1998–1999 season.

Carmelo was tall for his age as a high school freshman. But he needed to add weight before he was ready for the varsity basketball team.

NEW KID IN SCHOOL

Carmelo had been too skinny to make the varsity team as a freshman. "He was all arms and legs," said Towson basketball coach Mike Daniel. "He was like a string bean."

Carmelo shot up five inches between his freshman and sophomore seasons. He put on weight and got stronger. "Carmelo thought he was the best player on the court," said Coach Daniel. "He always does."

Carmelo made the varsity team as a sophomore. He had a good year. But he really turned it on during his junior season in 2000–2001. No one could stop him. Carmelo was six feet seven inches tall. He was strong. Carmelo was a tough defender. He grabbed rebounds. He could play any position on the court. And as always, he could score a lot of points.

Carmelo's favorite subject in high school was math. "I love working with numbers," he said.

Towson had a winning season in 2000–2001. Carmelo averaged more than 23 points and 10 rebounds

Carmelo *(far right, third row)* poses with his high school basketball team.

each game. He also made nearly four assists per game. People began to talk about what Carmelo would do after high school. Some of the best college basketball teams in the country showed interest in him.

Carmelo decided he wanted to go to Syracuse University. But he still had one more season of high school basketball to play. Towson is a good school. Carmelo had been treated well there.

But some people thought that Carmelo should transfer to Oak Hill Academy in Mouth of Wilson, Virginia. Oak Hill has one of the best high school basketball programs in the country.

Carmelo joined Oak Hill for the 2001–2002 season. He was a long way from home. But Carmelo's dream was to become the best basketball player possible. He was ready to work hard and take his game to the next level.

Carmelo looks to pass the ball during his season at Oak Hill.

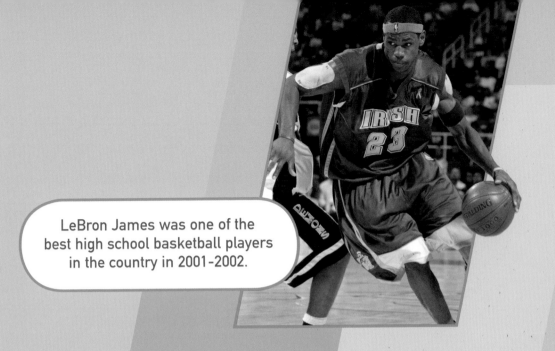

LeBron James was one of the best high school basketball players in the country in 2001-2002.

ORANGEMAN

The highlight of the 2001–2002 season at Oak Hill was a game against Ohio's St. Vincent-St. Mary (SVSM) High School. SVSM was one of the best teams in the country. Their star player was LeBron James. Most people thought James was the best high school player in the world. James and Carmelo had become friends at a basketball camp the previous summer.

17

Carmelo goes up for a basket.

The game between Oak Hill and SVSM was close. James scored 36 points. Carmelo scored 34. More importantly, Oak Hill won the game, 72–66. The fans stood and cheered when Carmelo came off the court.

"It was probably the best game I've been involved in as a high school coach," said Oak Hill coach Steve Smith.

Carmelo averaged more than 21 points and eight rebounds per game during his season with Oak Hill. He was ready for bigger challenges. Many people thought Carmelo could go straight to the NBA. He had the skills to compete with the world's best players.

Carmelo wanted to go to college. His mother was glad. She knew that her son's life would change when he became a pro basketball player. "I didn't want him to go to the NBA," Mary said. "I wanted my son to have a chance to be 18 years old."

Carmelo and his mother were both happy that the young star decided to go to college.

Carmelo *(with the ball)* made Syracuse a better team right away.

The Syracuse Orangemen have a long basketball history. Many future NBA stars played for Syracuse. Carmelo was named a starter for the 2002–2003 season. Coach Jim Boeheim wanted his star freshman on the court as much as possible. He knew that Carmelo might leave for the NBA after the season. "If Carmelo stays one year, that's better than no years," Coach Boeheim said.

Syracuse retired Carmelo's jersey number in a ceremony on February 23, 2013. No Syracuse player will be able to wear number 15 in the future.

Syracuse entered the **National Collegiate Athletic Association (NCAA) tournament** in March 2003. They made it all the way to the **Final Four**. Then the Orangemen beat the University of Texas and the University of Kansas. Carmelo and Syracuse were national champions!

Carmelo scored 20 points and grabbed 10 rebounds in the championship game. He was named Final Four Most Outstanding Player.

Carmelo dunks the ball during the NCAA tournament.

"We talked about him being the best player in the country," Coach Boeheim said of Carmelo after the game. "I think in this tournament, he proved it."

Carmelo *(center)* and the Orangemen celebrate their victory at the NCAA tournament!

Carmelo *(left)* and LeBron James were ready to join the NBA in 2003.

HOMECOMING

Two weeks after winning the national championship, Carmelo talked to reporters. "I'm here in front of you today to announce that I will not be coming back next year," Carmelo said with tears in his eyes. "I will be moving on, moving on to the pros."

The 2003 NBA **draft** was held on June 26. Melo's friend LeBron James was chosen by the Cleveland Cavaliers with the first pick. The Detroit Pistons held the second pick. They surprised many people by choosing Serbian **center** Darko Milicic. The Denver Nuggets chose next. They took Carmelo.

Carmelo and teammates celebrate a win against the Sacramento Kings.

The 2002–2003 Nuggets had won only 17 games. Things changed in 2003–2004 with Carmelo on the team. He scored 21 points per game. He made the players around him better. The team won 43 games and went to the **playoffs**. But Denver lost in the first round. Carmelo led the Nuggets to the playoffs seven years in a row. But they could not make it all the way to the **NBA Finals**.

Carmelo was named to the NBA **All-Star Game** for the first time during the 2006–2007 season.

Carmelo puts up a shot against the San Antonio Spurs.

Carmelo was to become a free agent after the 2010–2011 season. This meant he could join any team that wanted him. He wanted to play for his hometown New York Knicks. The Nuggets didn't want to wait for Carmelo to become a free agent. They traded him to the Knicks in the middle of the season.

Carmelo takes control of the ball during his first game with the Knicks.

Carmelo takes a shot.

Carmelo's first game with the Knicks was in New York on February 23, 2011. He scored 27 points as the crowd chanted, "Melo!, Melo!" The Knicks beat the Milwaukee Bucks, 114–108.

New York was good enough to enter the 2012–2013 playoffs. They faced the Boston Celtics in the first round. Carmelo hoped to make it to the NBA Finals for the first time.

Carmelo is happy to spend time with fans.

With Carmelo leading the way, the Knicks have a chance to be great. But Carmelo doesn't let his success go to his head. "Man, I'm not trying to be important," he said. "I just go out and play."

Selected Career Highlights

2012–2013 Named to NBA All-Star Game for sixth time

2011–2012 Named to NBA All-Star Game for fifth time
Finished sixth in the NBA in points per game (22.6)

2010–2011 Traded to New York Knicks during season
Named to NBA All-Star Game for fourth time
Finished third in the NBA in points per game (25.6)

2009–2010 Named to NBA All-Star Game for third time
Finished third in the NBA in points per game (28.2)

2008–2009 Finished seventh in the NBA in points per game (22.8)

2007–2008 Named to NBA All-Star Game for second time
Finished fourth in the NBA in points per game (25.7)

2006–2007 Named to NBA All-Star Game for first time
Finished second in the NBA in points per game (28.9)

2005–2006 Finished eighth in the NBA in points per game (26.5)

2004–2005 Finished 19th in the NBA in points per game (20.8)

2003–2004 Finished 12th in the NBA in points per game (21.0)
Chosen with the third pick in the NBA draft

2002–2003 Won national championship with Syracuse
Named Final Four Most Outstanding Player

2001–2002 Led Oak Hill Academy to winning record

Glossary

All-Star Game: a midseason game played by the best players in the NBA. Fans vote to decide who plays in the All-Star Game.

assists: passes to teammates that help teammates score baskets

asthma: a medical problem that affects a person's airways

borough: one of five political divisions of New York City. The boroughs are Brooklyn, the Bronx, Manhattan, Queens, and Staten Island.

center: a player who usually plays close to the basket. The center is usually the tallest player on the team.

defenders: players who try to keep the other team from scoring

draft: a yearly event in which sports teams take turns choosing new players

Final Four: the name given to the last four teams at the NCAA basketball tournament each year. The Final Four team that wins two more games becomes the national champion.

forward: a player who usually plays close to the basket

foul: to hit or push another player in a way that is against the rules. A player who is fouled often gets to shoot free throws.

free throw: a shot taken from behind the foul line on a basketball court. The other team cannot try to block a free throw.

layup: a shot taken with one hand close to the basket

National Collegiate Athletic Association (NCAA) tournament: a yearly tournament in which 65 teams compete to decide the national champion

NBA Finals: the last set of games in the NBA playoffs. The winner of the NBA Finals is the best team in the NBA for the season.

playoffs: a series of contests played after the regular season has ended

rebounds: grabbing missed shots

referee: a person who watches a game closely to make sure the rules are followed

varsity: the top sports team at a school

wide receiver: a football player whose main job is to catch passes

Further Reading & Websites

Kennedy, Mike, and Mark Stewart. *Swish: The Quest for Basketball's Perfect Shot*. Minneapolis: Millbrook Press, 2009.

Savage, Jeff. *LeBron James*. Minneapolis: Lerner Publications Company, 2012.

NBA Website
http://www.nba.com/
The NBA's website provides fans with news, statistics, biographies of players and coaches, and information about games.

Official Site of the New York Knicks
http://www.nba.com/knicks/
The official website of the Knicks includes schedules, news, and profiles of past and current players and coaches.

Official Website of Carmelo Anthony
http://thisismelo.com/
Learn more about Melo's life and career from his official website.

Sports Illustrated Kids
http://www.sikids.com/
The *Sports Illustrated Kids* website covers all sports, including basketball.

Index

Photo Acknowledgments

The images in this book are used with the permission of: Gary W. Green/MCT/Newscom, p. 4; © Sam Greenwood/Getty Images, pp. 5, 6; © Kim Klement-USA TODAY Sports, pp. 7, 8, 26; © euroluftbild.de/Glow Images, p. 9; © iStockphoto.com/Jeff Wilkinson, p. 10; Seth Poppel Yearbook Library, pp. 13, 15; © Kirby Lee/Image of Sport-USA TODAY Sports, pp. 16, 18; © Sporting News via Getty Images, p. 17; AP Photo/David Duprey, p. 19; TSN/Icon SMI STF/ TSN/Icon SMI/Newscom, p. 20; © Andy Lyons/Getty Images, p. 21; © Al Bello/Getty Images, p. 22; AP Photo/Frank Franklin ll, pp. 23, 27; AP Photo/Steve Yeater, p. 24; © Brian Bahr/Getty Images, p. 25; AP Photo/Kathy Willens, p. 28; © Jim McIsaac/Getty Images, p. 29.

Front Cover: © Jim McIsaac/Getty Images.

Main body text set in Caecilia LT Std 55 Roman 16/28.
Typeface provided by Adobe Systems.